DIY
Hand
LETTERING

FROM MONOGRAMMED PILLOWS
TO PERSONALIZED STATIONERY —

*25 handcrafted,
handlettered projects
you can make!*

MELISSA AVERINOS *and* ASHARAE KROLL

Aadamsmedia
Avon, Massachusetts

Published by
Adams Media, a division of F+W Media, Inc.
57 Littlefield Street, Avon, MA 02322. U.S.A.
www.adamsmedia.com

ISBN 10: 1-4405-8176-2
ISBN 13: 978-1-4405-8176-2
eISBN 10: 1-4405-8177-0
eISBN 13: 978-1-4405-8177-9

Printed in the United States of America.

10 9 8 7 6 5 4 3 2 1

Cover design by Stephanie Hannus.
Cover photography by Erin Dawson.
Handlettered alphabet art by Asharae Kroll.
Cover handlettered art by Asharae Kroll.
Interior photos by Melissa Averinos, Erin Dawson, and Stephanie Hannus.
Photo on page 136 by Asharae Kroll with Grain & Compass.

This book is available at quantity discounts for bulk purchases.
For information, please call 1-800-289-0963.

Dedicated, as always, to my Adorable Husband Stuart,

for believing in me until I believed in myself.

—Melissa

To my parents, for always encouraging me to create.

And to my husband Tim, for his unwavering love and support.

—Asharae

CONTENTS

Introduction

Have you ever seen interesting lettering on a piece of wall art or handmade card and wished you could make something like that? Guess what—you can! Even if you didn't get an A in penmanship in the second grade, you can learn a variety of beautiful handlettering styles that you can use to add personality to your next craft. Whether you want to make something for your home or to give as a gift, you'll find dozens of amazing options in this book.

In Part 1, we'll review the inexpensive and easy-to-find tools and materials you'll need to start handlettering. Then, you'll learn simple techniques to master several basic handlettering styles. Once you've got the hang of those, you can dig deeper and try some of the variations—small tweaks that add even more creativity to each style. You'll also find pages of fun flourishes and embellishments along with other ideas to add even more personality to your next project.

In Part 2, you'll find a range of unique crafts that will showcase your newly acquired handlettering skills. Tired of giving boring teacher gifts? Make a Lettered Mug with a quote about how valued teachers are. Want to freshen up your wall decor without spending a fortune? Whip up a painted Mirror—you can make it coordinate with any interior design style. Is your jewelry selection looking tired? Personalize a Statement Monogram Necklace and get ready to rake in the compliments.

LET'S GET STARTED!

PART 1
INTRO TO HANDLETTERING

Before we start crafting, it's important to learn a bit about the art of handlettering. Don't be intimidated by fancy-looking calligraphy or modern blocky styles—all of these options are easy to learn when you break down each letter into straight lines and curves. You'll learn several basic handlettering styles, plus dozens of variations to add new dimensions to each style. Whether you're looking for sophisticated, simple, whimsical, or artsy, you're sure to find a lettering style that you love!

Chapter 1
TOOLS OF THE TRADE

GETTING STARTED

You'll only need a few basic tools to jump into handlettering. Most are available at your local craft store or online, which makes it even easier to get started. Each project in Part 2 will list exactly what you need for that particular craft, but following is an overview of common handlettering tools and materials.

GOOD OL' PEN AND PAPER

Don't let materials intimidate you from trying a new handlettering craft! The truth is, you really only need a pencil or pen and a sheet of paper to get started. If you're overwhelmed at the prospect of increasing your crafting supplies, start slowly and just make a few projects with pen and paper first. Pilot G2 Premium Gel Roller Pens (1.0 mm) are a great place to start. Try making a simple greeting card, handlettering your favorite quote to put in a frame, or making a pretty menu for your next dinner party. Once you get comfortable doing a few handlettering styles with pen and paper, take it up a notch and invest in paint pens or some new brushes.

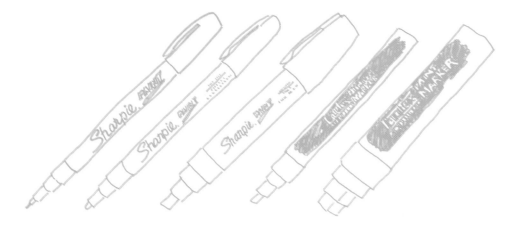

PAINT PENS

Using paint pens is one of the easiest ways to start lettering. They're simple to use, come in a lot of colors, and are inexpensive.

OIL-BASED

Sharpie Oil-Based Paint Markers, which run $3–$5 each, are a reliable, high-quality option. Use these when you want a glossy, opaque line. Generally, oil-based paint pens require shaking before use, similar to an aerosol spray paint can. These markers will usually say right on them that they are oil-based, but you can also tell by their fume-y smell.

Oil-based paint pens are available in bold, medium, fine, and extra-fine—but most stores only carry bold and medium, so you might need to look online for the full line of options.

WATER-BASED

Try Liquitex Professional Paint Markers, which are professional-quality water-based acrylic markers for artists. These "markers" are plastic tubes with a felt nib that are filled with liquid acrylic paint. They are available in a square-tipped 15 mm size (which makes a big and chunky line) and a 2 mm size, which has a smaller, chisel-like tip for finer writing.

BLEACH PENS

Bleach pens probably won't be at the craft store—instead, you'll find them in the laundry aisle of your local supermarket for about $6. I use the Clorox Bleach Pen Gel, the one that says "stain remover for whites." This product is in a plastic tube that has two tips: a small pen-like tip (which is the one you'll use) and a scrubby tip.

Since you'll be repurposing a household product for your own artistic uses, be careful with it. Use the bleach pen on 100% cotton fabric and make sure you have a piece of cardboard underneath it to protect the surface you are working on. Another tip: Experiment on scrap fabric to see for yourself how it works before starting on your project.

FABRIC PENS

We recommend the Stained by Sharpie Brush Tip Fabric Markers. An eight-pack of these will run you about $13. As the name says, they have a brush tip, which is especially nice for handlettering. As an added bonus, the ink in these pens resists fading on most fabrics during normal wash cycles.

For best results, use 100% cotton fabrics and machine-wash in cold water and hang them to dry. As always, when writing on your fabric, it's a good idea to have cardboard behind it in case it bleeds through to the back of the fabric.

WHAT DOES "RESIST" MEAN?

You know how when you paint a room you use painters' tape to protect the parts of the wall or trim that you *don't* want to get paint on? When the paint dries, you peel off the tape and reveal the untouched wall behind it. That's all a "resist" is. In this book, you'll use Pebeo Drawing Gum or washable school glue (instead of tape) on paper or fabric (instead of a wall). Once the layer of paint or dye dries, you then remove that "resist" and you're left with the original surface intact.

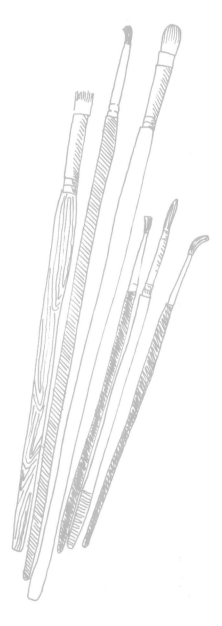

BRUSHES

You'll use different brush shapes, sizes, and materials for different paint types and applications. There are natural hair and synthetic, dozens of different names and shapes, and a wide range in price, from $2–$200! It'd be impossible to list the many brands and options out there. The best way to approach choosing brushes is to experiment and use what you like and what you can afford.

If you're not likely to take good care of your brushes, you might want to get the cheapest ones. You *should* care for your brushes, though, by washing them in water with mild soap right after use. This is not crucial when using watercolors, but acrylic paints will dry and harden your brush into a plastic nub if you don't wash them right away.

PROPER STORAGE OF TOOLS

Be sure to take good care of your handlettering tools and they will take care of you. Many paints and markers will last longer if stored in a cool, dry location—check the packaging for specific storage instructions. Be sure to store clean, dry brushes in a jar, handle-end down, or in some way that the bristles won't get smashed and misshapen while they're not in use. If you take a few minutes to clean up after each project, your materials will be ready to go the next time inspiration strikes.

ACRYLIC PAINTS

Acrylic paints are water-soluble and dry quickly. I like Golden and Liquitex brands. You'll use acrylic paints mainly on canvas and wood.

ACRYLIC PRIMER

This is the white paint that you prime surfaces with for further painting. It's sometimes called gesso. It creates a paintable, slightly porous surface that acrylic paint adheres to.

HIGH-FLOW VS. LOW-FLOW

Golden High Flow Acrylics have an ink-like consistency that makes them ideal for handlettering with a brush. Golden or Liquitex "heavy body" acrylics have a thicker, traditionally paint-like consistency and are better for covering large areas of wood or canvas.

ACRYLIC GEL MEDIUM

Use acrylic gel medium to dilute acrylic paint but keep the consistency close to regular paint. You can also use water to thin it as well, or a mixture of water and gel medium, but using the medium helps maintain the integrity of the paint, rather than just making it runny like plain water will.

ACRYLIC SEALER

Use acrylic sealer or varnish when you want to protect your painted surface or add a glossy finish to your final product.

Experimenting with Tools and Writing Surfaces

When you're getting started, try experimenting with a variety of tools and writing surfaces. You may find that some unusual surfaces make for great handlettering projects. Explore and see how each tool works, learn how it reacts on different surfaces, and discover which medium you enjoy best. If you're used to working with acrylics, get outside your comfort zone and try your hand at watercolors—you might discover that you enjoy crafting in a medium you've never tried before.

WATERCOLOR PAINTS

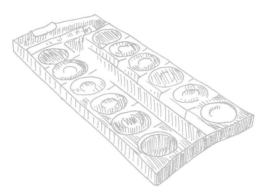

Watercolor paints are available in cakes/pans or in tubes. "Pan" watercolors are solid blocks of paint, which you wet with a brush to release the pigment. Tube watercolors have a pasty consistency. You squeeze out a little bit of pigment onto a palette and then dilute with water as desired. If you're just starting out, the pan type is the best option.

One good brand is Pelikan—their watercolors come in a set of twenty-four colors, which you can find for about $35. But if you're a beginner, you might be just as happy with a Crayola Washable Watercolors set of eight that you can get for about $5. If you fall in love with the medium, then move on to more expensive and higher-quality sets.

Watercolors are generally used on paper.

CERAMIC PAINT

Pebeo Porcelaine 150 water-based paints and paint pens are perfect for painting on ceramics. After letting your designs dry for 24 hours, you "fire" the ceramic item in a home oven at 300°F for 35 minutes. This creates a finish that's as permanent as baked enamel.

Technically, you aren't supposed to paint on a surface that will come into contact with food. So keep your designs focused on the outside of mugs or the edges of plates or on decorative items.

Practice, Practice, Practice

Some of the handlettering styles in this book can be a little tricky to get the hang of. Feel free to use tracing paper over each style in the book to trace the letters while you're learning. Keep practicing and don't get discouraged if your letters don't look the way you want—they'll get better over time. Once you're feeling confident with a style, put your own spin on it or create a new style entirely. The options are endless!

TOOLS FOR EMBOSSING AND ETCHING

Embossing and etching are two interesting ways to implement handlettering in a craft.

ETCHING CREAM

Since most of us don't have a sandblaster handy, which is the tool of choice for etching glass, we instead can use etching cream found in craft stores. Armour Etch is available in a 3-ounce bottle for about $10. This product contains hydrofluoric acid, which is corrosive to skin and irritating if inhaled, so be careful with it.

EMBOSSING PENS AND POWDERS

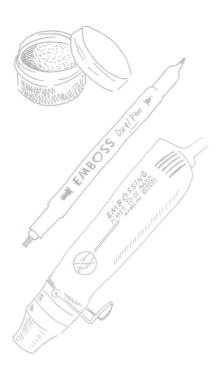

Embossing powder is finely ground plastic that melts quickly with a heat gun. It's used on paper for making cards or scrapbooking. You'll find this in the stamping section of your local craft store for less than $5 a jar.

The embossing pen or ink is simply something that stays wet long enough for the powder to stick to it and stay in place until you can melt the powder with a heat tool. Pigment inks are just as good for this as clear embossing pens, and the ink color ends up being covered by the opaque embossing powder anyway.

You'll also need a heat tool, which you can get for about $15. Nope, you can't use a hairdryer for this.

TOOLS FOR WOODBURNING

Woodburning is even more fun when you call it by its fancy name, *pyrography*, which translates from the Greek into "writing with fire."

You can get a woodburning tool for about $15 or a full starter kit for about $30 at your favorite craft and hobby store. The latter will come with a variety of metal tips that leave different shapes burned into the wood. You can achieve a large range of tones and shades with practice. Varying the type of tip used, the temperature, or the way the iron is applied to the material all create different effects.

In the same area of the craft store, you'll find soft, light-colored woods with fine grain (usually basswood and pine) to use in your projects.

DIGITIZING HANDLETTERING

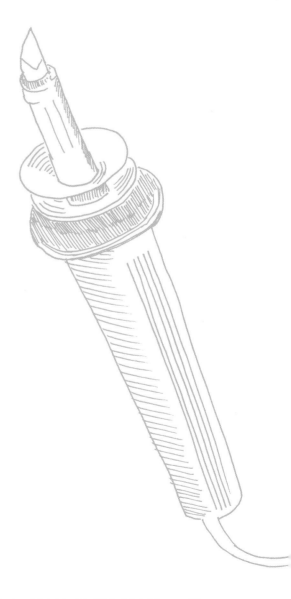

If you want to duplicate your work, scale it up to a larger size, or share it online, digitizing your handlettering is a great option. There are a myriad of tools available to help digitize your handlettering. If you're looking to jump straight to creating handlettering digitally, try using a Wacom Tablet (which connects with your computer) or an Apple Pencil (which works with an iPad Pro), or something similar.

If you prefer to create each style on paper first, all you need is a simple scanner that's big enough for the paper you're using. Scan at a high resolution, or a high dpi. The higher the dpi, the higher the quality of your scanned image, but also the larger your file size. A 600 dpi setting works well to scan detailed lettering and creates files that are a manageable size. You can use a program such as Adobe Photoshop to isolate your text, clean it up, and layer it with photos or other objects. If you want to scale your work up to a larger size, you'll need to turn your text into a vector. A vector will maintain the integrity of your lettering as you make it larger, rather than simply pixelating when you scale it up. Again, there are a variety of ways to do this—one being the Image Trace function in Adobe Illustrator. Styles done in black ink on white paper create the cleanest vectors for scaling to a larger size.

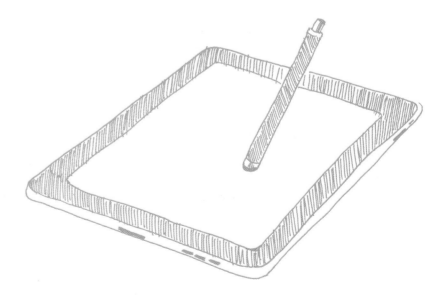

Chapter 2

BASIC HANDLETTERING STYLES

HOW TO BEGIN

This chapter provides an overview of several different handlettering styles. You can try them all, or pick and choose which ones to practice based on your own personal preferences. For each lettering style, you'll learn a bit about how to get started and you'll find practice pages where you can trace each letter of the alphabet. Once you feel comfortable tracing each style, you can try practicing it in your own hand.

No matter which handlettering style you decide to start with, you'll want to set up a workspace that will allow you to practice most effectively. For example:

- Clear off a table so you have enough elbowroom to move your arm freely.
- Be sure the table surface is clean and dry.
- Wash your hands.
- Turn on lighting that allows you to see what you're doing clearly without straining your eyes.

ABCDEFGHIJKLMN

TALL AND NARROW

HELPFUL HINT

While you're learning, it's helpful to use graph paper to get the hang of these proportions. If you make your letters two blocks wide and four blocks tall, they'll look great!

This handlettering style is fairly simple to do, so it's a good place to start. Sit up tall in your chair for this one! For this lettering style, it's important to aim for consistency. Make sure the vertical lines are truly vertical—no slanting vertical lines or wobbly lines.

You can play around with this style later to add more character to your project, but in the beginning, try playing by the rules. Make sure the tops and bottoms of your letters stay consistent as you write across the page.

In particular, pay close attention to where you cross your letters A and H—keep those lines high. The same goes for E and F—keep the middle line of the E and the bottom line of the F in the top ¼ of your overall letter height. The letters B, G, K, M, P, R, and Y also follow this rule, in their own way. The letters J and W do the opposite—the loop of the J only comes up to the bottom ¼ of your letter height, as does the middle point of the W.

OPQRSTUVWXYZ

If you pay attention to the details, you'll have this style mastered in no time. Pretty soon you'll be using it on invitations to your 1920s murder mystery party, the chalkboard menu board in your kitchen, or your fancied-up Christmas card envelopes.

Be sure to try your hand at combining this upright style with one that is a little more fluid and informal, such as the Cursive and Fake Calligraphy styles you'll see later in this chapter. For example, if you're handlettering a chalkboard menu for your kitchen, try writing "Menu" or "Tonight's Dinner" in a loose cursive at the top and use this tall, skinny style to list each of your menu items below. The contrasting styles complement one another very well.

HELPFUL HINT

The baseline refers to the imaginary straight line upon which each letter sits.

TALL AND NARROW VARIATIONS

Once you're ready to mix things up even more, try lengthening the right-hand diagonal lines of your letters A, K, and R below the baseline. Elongate your letters even more and create a moving baseline by writing some letters higher or lower than the others. By stretching each letter vertically or adding details and shading, you can create a whole new look.

ABCDEFGH

IJKLMNOPQ

RSTUVQRST

WXYZ

add curls to the ends of each letter

elongate beyond baseline

more than one stroke creates movement

create shadows

ABCDEFGHIJKLMNOPQRSTUVWXYZ

ABCDEFGHIJKLMNOPQRSTUVWXYZ

ABCDEFGHIJKLMNOPQRSTUVWXYZ

ABCDEFGHIJKLMNOPQRSTUVWXYZ

Practice, Practice, Practice

Practice, Practice, Practice

ABCDEFG OPQRSTU

BLOCKY SERIF

HELPFUL HINT

Visualize each letter before you begin—think about how much space it will take up, where the wide and the skinny parts of each letter will be, and be sure to leave enough space between letters for the serifs.

This lettering style takes a little more patience, but it's not difficult. The little doodads on the end of each letter are called serifs. (The other end of the lettering spectrum is called sans serif, or without serif.) The Tall and Narrow style you just learned is a good example of sans serif.

Serif styles in handlettering require more effort and planning to create, but they can make for some dramatic and beautiful results. This particular style requires a bit of forethought as you plan out your letter spacing and prepare for whatever project you have in mind.

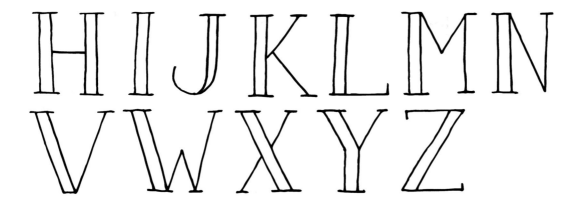

LETTERS WITH STRAIGHT LINES

Begin each letter that is comprised of straight lines (most of the alphabet) by drawing the two vertical or diagonal lines that make up the thicker side of the letter. The letter I is the simplest—draw your two vertical lines, then add the serifs at the top and bottom.

Now try the letter E. Draw your two vertical lines, for the thick edge of the letter. Next add the top line of the E—begin a little to the left of the vertical lines to give your letter a serif on the top left-hand side. Continue your horizontal line across and then add another serif detail on the right-hand side. Add in your bottom and middle lines of your E with respective serifs and you're done!

LETTERS WITH CURVES

Letters with a distinct curve to them require a different tactic. The letters C, G, J, O, Q, S, and U all fit this bill. O is probably the easiest of these letters to master—or perhaps the hardest if you have difficulty drawing a decent circle. Begin with the large circle of your letter O. After that, add the additional curved line on the inside that gives it the appearance of having a thicker side. For the other curved letters, begin with the outer shape of the letter, add your detail line on the inner curve that makes one section appear thicker, and then add your serifs.

BLOCKY SERIF VARIATIONS

Variations of this style are perfect for chalkboard lettering. Chalk is much more forgiving than pen and paper for a blocky lettering style like this one. You can also choose to add decorative details to the thick edge of your letters or simply color them in.

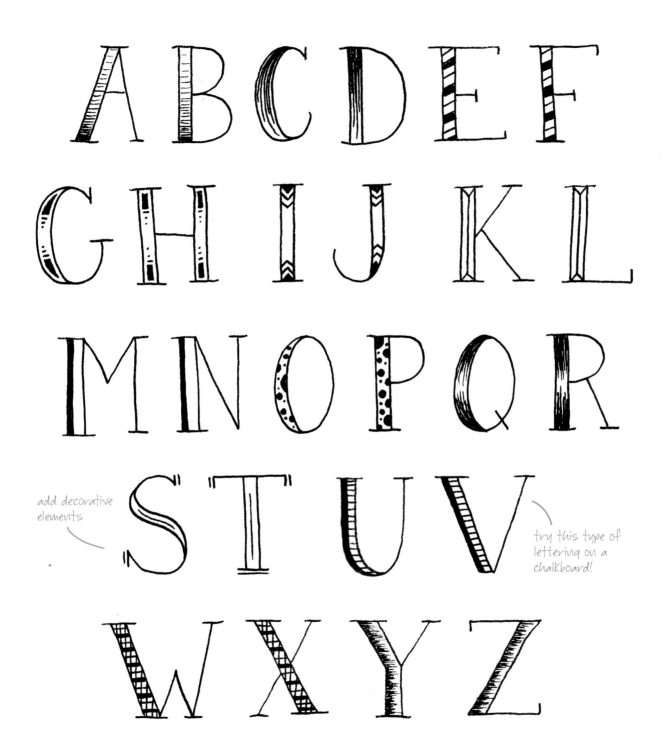

add decorative elements

try this type of lettering on a chalkboard!

ABCDEFGHIJKLM

NOPQRSTUVWXYZ

ABCDEFGHIJKLM

NOPQRSTUVWXYZ

ABCDEFGHIJKLM

NOPQRSTUVWXYZ

Practice, Practice, Practice

Practice, Practice, Practice

Aa Bb Cc Dd Ee
Ff Gg Hh Ii Jj Kk
Ll Mm Nn Oo Pp
Qq Rr Ss Tt Uu Vv
Ww Xx Yy Zz

PLAYFUL SERIF

This handlettering style is all about having fun with a traditional font. Imagine that the letters of a vintage typewriter hopped off the keyboard and had a dance party. This style is loosely based on that traditional typewriter style, which you'll notice in the distinct shape of the lowercase letters a and g as well as the capital letter Q. On the other hand, you'll see that the capital letters A, M, and N are fairly nontraditional.

This style is one of the easier ones to accomplish. It includes serif details like the Blocky Serif style, but the lines of each letter are simpler. Don't worry too much about making the heights of your letters perfectly even with one another. Feel free to give your words a more fluid look by dropping the tails for letters such as h, k, m, and n below the baseline.

This style would be great for signage at a casual outdoor wedding, a birthday card to your niece, or a custom welcome mat for your front door.

HELPFUL HINT

The key to this handlettering style is to make sure you don't take yourself too seriously. Have fun with it and try adding your own spin on each of the letters!

Playful Serif VARIATIONS

The variations of this style are endless. Since it has such an informal feel, you can add quirky details to make it even more fun. Try making your letters thicker, adding polka dots and curly ends to each letter, or create a new variation altogether.

Aa Bb Cc Dd Ee Ff

make your letters thicker

Gg Hh Ii Jj Kk Ll

Mm Nn Oo Pp Qq Rr

Ss Tt Uu Vv Ww

add quirky details

Xx Yy Zz

Aa Bb Cc Dd Ee Ff Gg Hh Ii Jj Kk Ll Mm

Nn Oo Pp Qq Rr Ss Tt Uu Vv Ww Xx Yy Zz

Aa Bb Cc Dd Ee Ff Gg Hh Ii Jj Kk Ll Mm

Nn Oo Pp Qq Rr Ss Tt Uu Vv Ww Xx Yy Zz

Aa Bb Cc Dd Ee Ff Gg Hh Ii Jj Kk Ll Mm

Nn Oo Pp Qq Rr Ss Tt Uu Vv Ww Xx Yy Zz

Practice, Practice, Practice

Practice, Practice, Practice

ABCDEFGHIJKLMN

BOLD AND BLOCKY

HELPFUL HINT

As you begin practicing each letter, make sure each line you draw is a consistent width. It's hardest to accomplish this on the curves, but with practice you'll get it right.

This handlettering style looks straightforward, but it's a little tricky to get right. There are several ways to accomplish this look, but I recommend using a thick marker with a flat edge, a wide calligraphy marker, chalk turned on its side, or any other writing utensil that has a wide, flat edge.

The simplest way to accomplish this style is to divide each letter into straight lines and curved lines. The letter W, for example, is a combination of four straight lines. The letter P is one straight line and one curved line. Breaking up each letter in this way will help you divide and conquer!

Pay close attention to the ends of each letter, and where your straight and curved lines meet one another. To make your lettering neat and consistent, the ends of each letter should stop on a horizontal or vertical line, and your outer corners should meet at around a 90-degree angle.

OPQRSTUVWXYZ

The letter E is a good example of both of these "rules." Note how the three horizontal lines of the E meet the vertical line at a neat 90-degree angle, and the ends of each horizontal line stop on a neat vertical edge as well.

How well you execute the letters C, G, J, and S will make a big difference in how consistent your lettering looks. Be sure to end the curved lines of each of those letters on a horizontal edge, rather than a diagonal. This takes practice—don't get discouraged!

C *instead of* C

G *instead of* G

J *instead of* J

S *instead of* S

BOLD AND BLOCKY
VARIATIONS

Once you've mastered the basics of this style, you can add loads of variations, shading, and other details to spice up your handlettering. Hint: you can even break the previous rules and purposely end each letter with diagonal edges to loosen up the look of your project. Use a thin marker or a contrasting paint color to add dots or zigzagging lines atop each letter to add interest. This style would also look great combined with one that is loose and flowy, such as the Cursive or Fake Calligraphy styles you'll find later in this chapter. Try making a birthday card for a friend by lettering "Happy Birthday" in this big, bold style and "to you" below it in tiny cursive lettering. How cute would that be?

ABCD EFGH

add shading

IJKL MNOPQ

use a contrasting color for dots!

RSTUV WXYZ

ABCDEFGHIJKLMNOPQRSTUVWXYZ

ABCDEFGHIJKLMNOPQRSTUVWXYZ

ABCDEFGHIJKLMNOPQRSTUVWXYZ

Practice, Practice, Practice

Practice, Practice, Practice

abcdefghijklmnopqrstuvwxyz

CURSIVE

As you practice this handlettering style, imagine yourself back in third grade—relearning the basics of cursive handwriting on lined paper. Feel free to actually use lined paper while you're starting out! Or, you can lay tracing paper on top of lined paper for some guidelines that won't show up on your practice sheet. If you like, you could also trace the alphabet on these pages until you get used to the look and feel of each letter.

Keep practicing and you'll get the hang of this basic cursive style. You won't even have to endure questionable cafeteria food or risk getting cooties to do so.

cursive VARIATIONS

Once you've mastered the basics of this standard cursive lettering, start to experiment a little more with it. Spread out your letters, slant them more or less, use a thicker or thinner pen, add extra loops in the letters s and r, or drop some of your letters lower or lift them higher to give your writing a moving baseline. Remember, this is *handlettering*—it doesn't have to be perfect!

a b c d e f
ghijk lmnop
qrstuv wxyz

abcdefghijklmnopqrstuvwxyz

abcdefghijklmnopqrstuvwxyz

abcdefghijklmnopqrstuvwxyz

Practice, Practice, Practice

abcdefghijklmn

FAKE CALLIGRAPHY

Calligraphy is an art form all its own. With endless variations and a range of difficulty levels, you could truly spend years perfecting this art. If you have the time and the urge to practice true calligraphy, go for it! It's beautiful and so very rewarding.

For our purposes, we'll build off of the cursive lettering style you just learned in order to create a style that imitates calligraphy. This style doesn't even require any special pens, nibs, or inks to create. Since many of us don't have the time to pick up another new hobby, this handlettering style is the perfect compromise.

Calligraphy is, in a most basic description, made up of thick and thin lines. A calligraphy pen is specifically designed to control the flow of ink to make those thick and thin lines. The nib (the special type of tip on calligraphy pens) lets out a small amount of ink as you make an upward stroke. When you make a downward stroke, the nib opens slightly, letting out more ink and creating a thicker line. If you're completely new to calligraphy, take a close look at the alphabet illustrated previously and visualize yourself tracing each letter. You'll notice that each upward stroke is a thin line and each downward stroke is a thick line.

Begin each word by writing the basic cursive version with an ordinary pen. Once you've finished the word, go back and add a thicker

o p q r s t u v w x y z

edge to each of your downward strokes. Depending on how dramatic you'd like your look to be, you can adjust the thickness of your downward strokes to be subtle or more intense.

Take a look at the letters here. The arrows on the letters a, b, and c indicate each downward stroke. Those downward strokes are where you'll thicken your letters to create the appearance of calligraphy. When you're practicing, write each word in cursive, then add some extra weight to each downward stroke by drawing in an extra line beside your downward strokes and coloring in the space between those lines. It'll get easier with practice!

abc

abc

abc

fake calligraphy VARIATIONS

You can completely change the feel of your lettering by adjusting the slant and spacing of your letters. Try making your letters formal and upright. Or, you can create a fun look by varying the slant of each letter and creating a moving baseline. Stretch out your letters, add extra loops and details, or stop before coloring in the downward strokes to leave your lettering open and airy.

abcdef ghijk

lmnop

qrstuv wxyz

abcdefghijklm

nopqrstuvwxyz

abcdefghijklm

nopqrstuvwxyz

abcdefghijklm

nopqrstuvwxyz

Practice, Practice, Practice

Practice, Practice, Practice

abcdef
ghijklm
nopqrs
tuvwxyz

BRUSH SCRIPT

This style takes quite a bit of practice to accomplish. It's different from the styles we've learned so far because it requires a brush rather than a pen. When you're starting out, use a brush with long, thin bristles. Different sizes, lengths, and types of bristles will give you different results.

Give yourself plenty of time and practice to get used to this style. It feels different from writing with a pen, but the results will be well worth the work. In some ways, this style is similar to calligraphy—pressing the brush down harder on each downward stroke will result in a thicker line, and lightly drawing the brush upward will create thin lines.

It's a good idea to use special watercolor paper for this style if you're using watercolors or a watery ink such as calligraphy ink to paint your letters. This thicker paper is more absorbent and won't curl up as some thinner papers will when laden with wet paint. If you would like to use this style on wood or some other hard surface, try using acrylic paints instead. This will give each letter a heavier, more consistent look, rather than the whimsical look that watercolors have.

HELPFUL HINT

Remember to reload your brush with more paint before starting each letter when using watercolors. This will offer beautiful variation in the tones of each letter.

brush script VARIATIONS

Once you're ready to take this style to the next level, try these ideas:

- Use different brush sizes and bristle types to vary the feel of your lettering.
- Experiment with a flowy, loopy lettering style or try one that is more upright and formal.
- Combine two complementary paint colors on your brush to vary the look of each letter.
- Paint your lettering with a liquid masking fluid (such as Pebeo Drawing Gum, available at art supply and craft stores) and then paint a wash over the letters to give the lettering a colorful background. Check out the Watercolor-Resist Artwork craft in Chapter 5 for more instructions.

ABCD
efgh
ijkl mnopq
rstuv
WXYZ

abcdefghijklm

nopqrstuvwxyz

abcdefghijklm

nopqrstuvwxyz

abcdefghijklm

nopqrstuvwxyz

Practice, Practice, Practice

Practice, Practice, Practice

CHOOSING A LETTERING STYLE THAT'S RIGHT FOR YOUR PROJECT

Once you're ready to start crafting, it's important to choose a handlettering style that fits the vibe of your project. Try choosing descriptive words that convey the feeling you want to have when you look at your craft. From there, pick a lettering style that fits your description.

Want to create a greeting card that feels bright, fun, and happy? Choose a style such as the Bold and Blocky style or the Playful Serif style. Creating signage for a friend's fancy wedding? Choose a romantic, elegant lettering style such as the Cursive style or Fake Calligraphy style. Want to create a quirky welcome mat with a funny saying on it? Use one of the decorative variations of the Blocky Serif style. If you haven't learned a style that's just perfect for your project, use the ones you find here as inspiration to create your own.

Chapter 3
TAKING YOUR HANDLETTERING A STEP FURTHER

ADDING DETAILS

In this chapter, you'll find a variety of doodles, embellishments, flourishes, and other ideas you can incorporate into your handlettering. You can use these fun details to add extra personality to any project. Just like the handlettering styles we learned in the last chapter, you're welcome to lay tracing paper over the pages here to get a feel for each flourish and doodle. You can also simply use these embellishments as inspiration and create your own style to go with the craft you're making. At the end of this chapter you'll find ideas and encouragement to think outside the box and create your own lettering styles and decorative details.

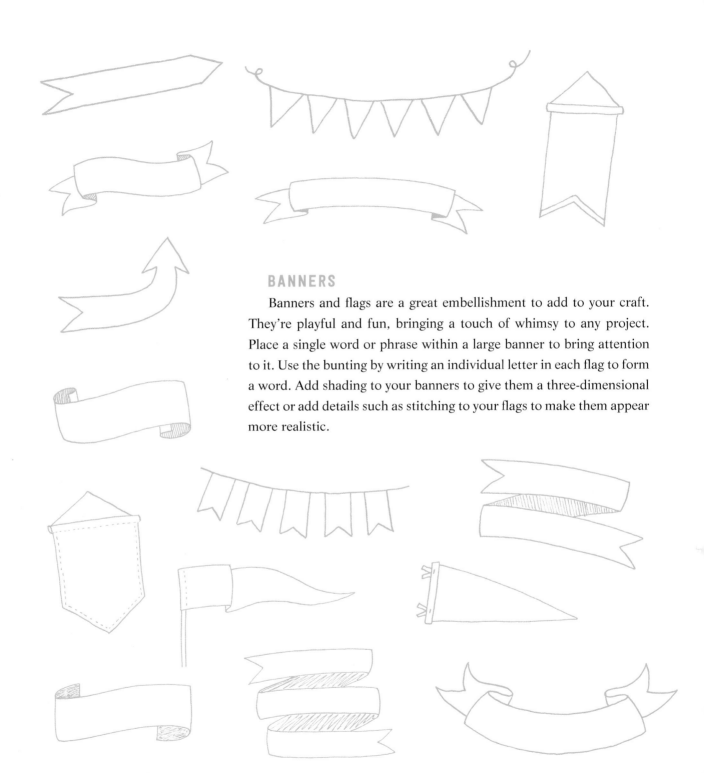

BANNERS

Banners and flags are a great embellishment to add to your craft. They're playful and fun, bringing a touch of whimsy to any project. Place a single word or phrase within a large banner to bring attention to it. Use the bunting by writing an individual letter in each flag to form a word. Add shading to your banners to give them a three-dimensional effect or add details such as stitching to your flags to make them appear more realistic.

CORNERS

Adding decorative corners around your handlettering can draw attention in toward the text you place in the center. Corners are ideal for a project that is intended to be square or rectangular. You can use a singular corner to add just a touch of detail to your project, use two of these designs in opposite corners for an asymmetrical look, or surround your lettering with decorative corners on all sides to form a border all the way around.

The corners you'll find here were inspired by art deco architecture and things you find in nature. Try looking around your house or your neighborhood to find inspiration and create your own decorative corner details.

LINES AND SWIRLS

If you're looking for a way to create a border around your project or to separate lines of text, drawing decorative lines into your handlettering project is a great solution. Here are a few ideas to get you started. Feel free to add your own twist on the decorative lines featured here.

Adding swirls and curls to your project is sure to make it feel fun and whimsical. You can use these doodles to underline your lettering, emphasize certain words, or simply add some decorative elements to a project.

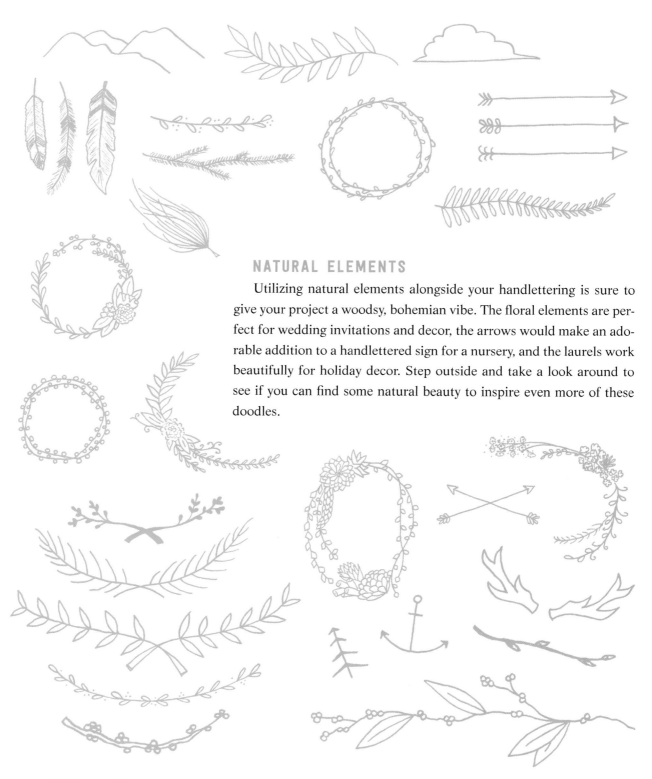

NATURAL ELEMENTS

Utilizing natural elements alongside your handlettering is sure to give your project a woodsy, bohemian vibe. The floral elements are perfect for wedding invitations and decor, the arrows would make an adorable addition to a handlettered sign for a nursery, and the laurels work beautifully for holiday decor. Step outside and take a look around to see if you can find some natural beauty to inspire even more of these doodles.

abcd

EFGH

ijkl

MNOPQ

ADDING SHADOWS TO YOUR LETTERING

Shadows are a great way to give your lettering more depth and to make it appear as if it's jumping off the page. There are a few ways to accomplish this, depending on the lettering style you've chosen and the final look you'd like it to have. To give your lettering consistent shadows, imagine you're pointing a flashlight at each word. This works best if you "point the flashlight" at your lettering from one of the corners—the top right corner, for example. Visualize where the shadow would fall underneath your letters and draw it in. You can draw this shadow in beneath your lettering as a thin line for a delicate look, a thick line for a more intense shadow, hatching (tiny parallel lines) or crosshatching (tiny perpendicular lines) for an illustrative feel, or any other way you can dream up. Be sure to handletter your words first, then add in your shadow details afterward.

RSTUV

wxyz

WHERE TO FIND ADDITIONAL INSPIRATION

Once you start digging into the art of handlettering, you may find yourself wanting to learn more techniques and lettering styles. If you look around, you'll see inspiration for new lettering styles and decorative elements everywhere! Take a walk through your neighborhood and look at the lettering on shop signs and house numbers, the architectural details on older buildings, and even the flowers growing out of the sidewalk. Hop over to your local library or bookstore to browse through book covers for lettering inspiration. Thrift stores are also a fabulous place to collect ideas for handlettering projects. Old labels, vintage postcards, cigar boxes, and old maps can provide beautiful ideas for your next project. Take photos of everything that strikes your fancy and keep a collection of these ideas to inspire your next handlettering project!

NEXT STEPS

Now that you have a solid foundation of lettering styles and embellishments in your repertoire, you can decide which options best fit your personality, decor preferences, and crafting choices. There are no right answers! The handlettering styles for each craft in Part 2 show just one way to do each project. Don't feel obligated to make your project look the same as the ones you find here—feel free to customize however you like. A project can take on a totally different feel depending on which lettering style and decorative elements you choose, so the options are endless.

Now, it's time to start crafting!

PART 2

HANDLETTERING PROJECTS

In this section you'll put your new lettering skills to use in a wide variety of crafts. Remember, the designs shown here are just jumping-off points—you can change colors and lettering styles to make each craft truly one of a kind. Each one is simple enough for any beginning crafter to tackle. In fact, the toughest part is deciding which one to try first!

Chapter 4
KITCHEN

In this chapter, you'll find handlettering projects for the heart of the home, the kitchen. If your kitchen staples, such as napkins, glassware, and mugs, could use some sprucing up, these crafts will turn them into conversation pieces the next time you have a get-together. Let's get cooking!

UPCYCLED NAPKINS

Do you have a bunch of plain T-shirts lying around that you don't wear often? (Doesn't everyone?) Upcycle them into some cute, no-sew napkins! If you haven't dyed anything before, this is a quick way to try your hand at it on something you might throw away anyway. The glue-resist technique looks difficult but it couldn't be easier.

YOU WILL NEED:

- ☐ 100% cotton adult-sized T-shirts in light colors, without any printing or decorations on them (1 shirt will yield 2 napkins)
- ☐ Ironing board (or use a table with a folded towel on it)
- ☐ Iron
- ☐ Scissors
- ☐ Freezer paper
- ☐ Optional: scrap paper and pencil

- ☐ Elmer's Washable No Run School Glue
- ☐ Elmer's Washable School Glue Stick
- ☐ Rubber gloves
- ☐ Fabric dye (color of choice)
- ☐ Bin for dyeing
- ☐ Mild soap
- ☐ Old toothbrush

1   Turn the T-shirt inside out and lay it on top of the ironing board. Arrange it so both layers of the shirt lie nice and flat.

2   Iron the T-shirt to remove any wrinkles or creases.

3   Cut 18" × 18" squares of freezer paper for as many napkins as you plan to make.

4   Place a piece of freezer paper, shiny side down, onto the wrong side of the T-shirt and iron evenly over the paper. The plastic coating on the freezer paper will warm up and make a temporary bond with the cotton. This gives you stability when you letter on the fabric and also keeps the glue from seeping through and sticking to your table.

5   Flip over the shirt and repeat step 4 with another piece of freezer paper. Repeat for as many napkins as you wish to make.

6   Cut the freezer-papered squares of fabric from the T-shirts. You will now have squares of fabric with right side of the T-shirt fabric facing up and freezer paper ironed to the back.

7   Practice your lettering on scrap paper with a pencil if desired. Keep in mind that you want some "space" within the letters and between them because the glue will spread a little.

8   Take your time and draw on your letters with the glue. See the sidebar for tips. Let the glue dry completely; overnight is ideal. Peel off the backing paper.

9   Wearing gloves, prepare the dye in a bin according to the manufacturer's instructions. Submerge the napkins in the dye and let soak for as long as you like, depending on how dark you want them to get.

10 Carefully remove the napkins from the dye bath and rinse thoroughly. Then, while running the napkins under warm water with a little bit of mild soap, scrub off the glue with the toothbrush.

11 Rinse thoroughly and air-dry, or run through the washer and drier.

12 You'll probably notice that the edges of the fabric have taken care of themselves by curling in slightly. If you'd like them to curl more, just give each edge of the napkins a gentle tug.

VARY THE GLUE TYPES

The glue stick and the liquid glue will create different looks, so mix them up as desired. For fewer words that are bold, use the glue stick, going over it a couple of times. For finer letters, use the liquid glue. Embrace the imperfections that will inevitably happen, as the more you try to fix it, the worse it will look. Just go with it and have fun—it doesn't have to be perfect!

ELIXIR
~ of ~
LIFE

NECTAR
of the
GODS

LETTERED MUGS

Melissa's love for her morning cup of coffee inspired this handlettered project. Once you get your hands on some Pebeo Paint Markers—made especially for permanently painting on ceramic—no mug will be safe near you. This project has endless variation possibilities and makes a perfect gift.

YOU WILL NEED:

- [ ] Optional: scrap paper and pencil
- [ ] White mugs
- [ ] Black Pebeo Porcelaine 150 Paint Markers, thin and thick tips
- [ ] Precision-tip cotton swabs (look for them in the makeup aisle) or cotton balls
- [ ] Acetone nail polish remover

1 Practice your lettering and layout on scrap paper with a pencil if desired.

2 Clean and thoroughly dry the mugs. Use the bold pen to write the large words and the fine pen to write the smaller words as in the images here. Take your time with the lettering and think about "dragging" the paint on the surface of the mug like you would apply nail polish, rather than painting "into" the mug. If you want more coverage, resist the temptation to go right over it again and wait for it to dry first.

3 You can easily remove any mistakes with a cotton swab or cotton ball dipped in acetone. Make sure to wipe off *all of what you want removed*—don't leave smears or they will bake on. Let the acetone evaporate before trying again with the paint pen.

4 Once the first coat is completely dry, go over any thin areas and finish ends of letters if needed. This is the time to personalize the project with your own design sense, so add decorative flourishes or swirls as desired. As before, use the acetone to correct mistakes.

5 Let dry for 24 hours. Cure in your home oven according to the pen manufacturer's instructions (see the sidebar).

YOU NEED SPECIAL PENS!

The Internet sometimes lies. For example, it claims that you can use a basic Sharpie marker on ceramic and then bake it in your oven so it stays on permanently. Sorry to burst your bubble: That doesn't work. Pebeo Porcelaine 150 Paint Markers are formulated specifically for creating a permanent finish on ceramic and glass. You have to let them air-dry for 24 hours and then bake them at 300°F in your home oven for 35 minutes. Don't preheat! You want to put them in a cold oven and then turn on the heat, which allows the ceramic and paint to warm up gradually. Once the 35 minutes has passed, turn off the heat and allow the decorated mug to cool down in the oven, only removing it once it has reached room temperature.

Once dried and heat-set, the durable, high-gloss finish is permanent, but not food safe—so don't paint inside a mug or on the face of a plate. Once cured, the paint is also dishwasher safe, but it's better to just hand wash it because it will last longer that way.

VARIETY

may be the spice of life, but

basil

is the herb of

PESTO

BASIL POTS

Decorating terra cotta pots is an inexpensive and fun way to add personality to your decor. All it takes is some simple whitewashing followed by handpainted lettering. These also make excellent hostess gifts, especially when planted with herbs.

1. Whitewash the pots by painting with a wet brush dipped into a little bit of white paint. It's okay if this looks messy or drippy—just smooth the watered-down paint over the pot. To keep a rustic, whitewashed look, you want to be able to see the terra cotta color through the paint. Let dry completely.

2. Practice your lettering and layout on scrap paper if desired. Lightly pencil in the lettering on the pot.

3. Paint on the letters with black high-flow acrylic paint and a fine brush. Take your time and enjoy the process. Go back and neaten up any edges and add flourish details if you like. Let dry. If desired, seal with a coat of spray acrylic sealer.

4. Place your herb plant inside (still in its own plastic pot) and you are good to go!

YOU DON'T EVEN HAVE TO REPOT THE PLANT!

Terra cotta is porous, so unless you seal it really well, the moisture from watering the plant will inevitably seep through the pot. This may affect your decoration by discoloring it or making the paint peel. To avoid this (and the need to deal with multiple coats of sealer), I like to use the plastic pots that the plants come in and just pop those right into the terra cotta pots, plant and all. This will keep the moisture from wicking out to the terra cotta and your designs will stay in great shape.

SPOON REST

Who doesn't love to spoon? It's so easy to transform a plain ceramic dish into this cheeky Spoon Rest—all you need are Pebeo Porcelaine 150 Paints and Paint Markers. (See the sidebar for more information on these special paints.)

1 Practice your design on paper with a pencil if desired. Try the same word in different letter types and experiment with adding borders or decorative touches.

2 Practice a little on the underside of the dish with the paint. It has a different consistency than many other kinds of paint. Get a feel for how much paint you need to get on the brush to get the kind of coverage you like. Once you feel ready to move on, simply wipe off your practice with a cotton swab or cotton ball soaked in acetone.

3 Take your time and paint your letters on the dish with a brush, or use the Pebeo Porcelaine 150 Paint Markers.

4 Don't worry about making a mistake because you can just wipe it away with the acetone.

5 Draw in the spoon shapes and then go back with a paint pen and add face details.

6 Use paint and a brush to add the border.

7 Let dry and bake according to the paint manufacturer's instructions (see sidebar for Lettered Mugs for more information).

8 Optional: If you'd like to add a base to the plate so it doesn't scratch your oven or countertop, cut cork sheeting to fit the base of the dish and use Gorilla Glue to adhere.

MORE IDEAS

Once you own some Pebeo Porcelaine 150 Paints and Paint Markers, you will want to decorate everything you can get your hands on! Here are a few ideas for you, using these same instructions:

- Enhance a plain vase with a quote about flowers.

- Paint your monogram on 4" × 4" ceramic tiles to use as coasters. You'll definitely want to glue cork sheeting to the bottom of these so they don't scratch your table.

- Transform a boring canister into a treat jar for your favorite canine by handlettering your dog's name in a phrase like "Max is a GOOD BOY!" (Max is Melissa's puppy's name, and yes, he is a good boy, mostly.)

- Make a charming winter gift for a neighbor by adding a quote about tea to a small teapot. A couple of suggestions: "A cup of tea would restore my normality." (Douglas Adams) or "But indeed I would rather have nothing but tea." (Jane Austen)

- Monogram egg cups with a family's initials, in a different color for each person.

- Write the whole alphabet around the rim of a boring white bowl and look at that, it's an educational tool!

ETCHED WINEGLASSES

Whether you use them for wine or water, we all have glasses that could use some sprucing up. Customizing glasses with etching cream is a simple way to bring your own style to the table. Cheers!

YOU WILL NEED:

- [ ] Optional: scrap paper and pencil
- [ ] Wineglasses
- [ ] Oil-based paint pen (color of choice)
- [ ] Precision-tip cotton swabs or cotton balls
- [ ] Acetone nail polish remover
- [ ] Rubber gloves and protective eyewear
- [ ] Etching cream (see Chapter 1)
- [ ] Paintbrush

1   Practice your design on scrap paper with a pencil if desired.

2   Draw on the glasses with a paint pen.

3   Remove mistakes if necessary with acetone and cotton swabs or cotton balls.

4   Add any other decorative elements you like.

5   Once you have your design drawn on completely, use protective gear (gloves, eyewear) and open the jar of etching cream. To apply it to the glass, think about almost "frosting" the glass (no pun intended) the way you might frost a cake. Drag a thick layer of cream across the design, rather than brushing it on thinly. I like to use a thicker border of paint pen resist to remind me where to stop when applying the cream. Leave the glass beyond the thick border lines unpainted. This will give you a clean edge of etching once the cream is rinsed off.

6   Let it sit for 5 minutes and then carefully rinse off the cream. The paint pen lettering will come right off too. If some of the thick border paint remains, remove it with acetone and a cotton ball. The etching won't look like much until the glass is totally dry, but then you'll see your design come to life!

ETCHING TIP

Etching cream is easy to find and simple to use, but it does have some limitations. If you tried to do a large area of etching, you'd see that it's hard to get it to look consistent. To avoid this problem, I like to use a lot of resist—in this case the paint pen—and make only small areas that need to be etched.

Chapter 5
WALL ART

You don't have to go to an expensive home decor store to get cool art for your walls; in this chapter, you'll learn how to make your own! Plus, you'll likely find that when you invest your time and love into making something, it has more meaning than something manufactured. You'll get to show off your handlettering and great taste when your walls are covered with these projects using inspiring quotes and sweet words.

FAUX CHALKBOARD

Black foam core and some white paint pens are all you need to quickly create chalkboard-inspired wall decor. Add some fun cord as a hanger and you're done. Best of all, it's chalk dust–free!

1. To start, draw a thick line around the perimeter of the foam core with the wide-tip marker. Pretend you are writing on a real chalkboard and don't worry about making it perfectly straight.

2. Use the thinner marker to add decorative details to or around the thick border. Some suggestions: add dots, spirals, or hearts to the space between the edge of the foam core and the line you drew in step 1. Or, add a scalloped look by drawing semicircles along the existing line. You can also keep it super simple and echo the bold line with a thinner one.

3. If desired, practice your lettering first on a scrap piece of paper to figure out the spacing and layout. Once you are happy with that, lightly pencil it on the foam core. Make sure to leave a good margin between the lettering and the border so the words have "space" and don't look cramped.

4. Draw on top of the penciled-in lettering with the thinner paint pen. Slow movement will give you better coverage, but it's totally fine to do it quickly for a more fluid application.

5. If some areas are too light, simply go back over it with the marker to thicken up the paint.

6 Once the paint is completely dry, erase any remaining pencil lines.

7 Using the toothpick, poke holes in the top corners of the foam core. Gently push the awl into the holes to widen them uniformly.

8 Thread the cord through and knot each end to make a hanger.

OTHER IDEAS

Not into cake? Weird, but to each her own. Perhaps you'd like to make this project for the living room or bedroom instead of the kitchen. Just pick a quote that coordinates to the location and go for it! Here are some ideas to get you started:

For the bedroom, try quotes about sleep:

"NO DAY IS SO BAD IT CAN'T BE FIXED WITH A NAP."

—Carrie Snow

"WE ARE SUCH STUFF AS DREAMS ARE MADE ON; AND OUR LITTLE LIFE IS ROUNDED WITH A SLEEP."

—Shakespeare

"MY FORMULA FOR LIVING IS QUITE SIMPLE. I GET UP IN THE MORNING AND I GO TO BED AT NIGHT. IN BETWEEN, I OCCUPY MYSELF AS BEST I CAN."

—CARY GRANT

For the living room, you could look up quotes for "home," "family," or something related to your pets or a favorite hobby. One good resource is *www.brainyquote.com*.

WOODBURNED LOVERS' PLAQUE

This simple woodburning project is an elegant riff on the tradition of sweethearts carving their initials into a tree. Take some time to practice on the scrap wood first, and in no time you'll be a woodburning pro. Choose your letter style carefully with this project. If you are comfortable with burning thin, curved lines, then feel free to use those kinds of letters in your design. If not, choose a bolder option.

YOU WILL NEED:

- ☐ Woodburning tool
- ☐ Ceramic mug (to use as a heat-safe holder for the tool)
- ☐ Scrap wood
- ☐ Scrap paper
- ☐ Pencil
- ☐ Wooden plaque tree slice (available at craft stores)
- ☐ Sawtooth hanger
- ☐ Gorilla Glue
- ☐ 2 rubber bumpers (available in the picture-framing section of craft stores)

1 First, let's practice. Place the tip-end of the woodburning tool in the mug and plug it in. Practice writing on the scrap wood. Take your time. This will help you get a sense of how long to hold the tool on the wood, how hard to press, and what kind of marks are created by holding the tool at different angles. Some tools come with different metal tips to attach to get different line qualities. Try it all out to see how it feels.

2 Now, plan out your design on paper.

3 Pencil in that design on the tree slice.

4 Using the woodburning tool, burn over your penciled-in lines.

5 Glue the hanger onto the back. Adhere the bumpers to the bottom of the back of the plaque as needed using Gorilla Glue to help the tree slice lie flat against the wall.

FIFTH-ANNIVERSARY GIFT

Customize this project as a wedding gift or for a fifth anniversary, which traditionally calls for a gift made of wood. Try incorporating a featured flower or motif from the happy couple's ceremony and add the date curved around the bottom edge of the wood. Instead of initials, you could use a phrase from their vows, first-dance song, or words from a toast made in their honor.

people will forget
WHAT YOU SAID.
people will forget
WHAT YOU DID.
but people will
never forget
how you made
them feel.

~maya angelou

CANVAS QUOTE

This handlettered canvas is the perfect way to keep your favorite quote right in front of you, where it can inspire you daily. These make a quick and thoughtful gift—just keep a few canvases on hand and customize with text that is meaningful to the recipient.

YOU WILL NEED:

- [ ] Acrylic paints (colors of choice)
- [ ] Optional: scrap paper
- [ ] Scrap cardboard (to use as a palette)
- [ ] Paintbrush
- [ ] Stretched canvas
- [ ] Paint pen (color of choice; I like Sharpie Oil-Based Paint Markers for this project)
- [ ] Pencil

1   Choose which colors you'll use. I like to use two colors that blend into each other well, which creates a lovely shifting color rather than a flat, solid look. If you aren't sure how your colors will look when they mix, test them out on a piece of scrap paper. Once you've decided on your colors, squeeze some of each onto your scrap cardboard palette.

2   Using your paintbrush, grab some of one color and smear it onto the canvas, then repeat with the other color. This is just to get the paint on the canvas. You don't have to worry about coverage yet and you don't even have to wash the brush between colors.

3   Now have fun smooshing the different colors of paint around on the canvas. You don't want to completely mix them so that it's one solid color—let them blend in some places and be their original color in other places. You might like to get your brush wet to help the paint spread and mix. Make sure to paint the sides of your canvas.

4   Let the canvas dry completely.

5   You might want to test out different paint pen colors on the folded-over canvas on the back of the stretcher bars to be sure you know how the lettering will appear against your background.

6 If desired, practice your lettering on scrap paper to figure out the best spacing and layout. Lightly pencil in your lettering on the canvas, to serve as a guide, then go over it with the paint pen. If you feel bold, just go for it now with your paint pen. Add flourishes to the outer edges of the canvas for added flair.

7 To avoid stretching out the canvas, try not to press too hard with the pen. If you do find the canvas is a little "loose" after you've finished, run a washcloth under hot water and moisten the canvas fabric from the back. Let it dry completely. This will shrink up the canvas, making it taut once again.

GETTING FULL COVERAGE WITH PAINT PENS

Keep in mind that some of the paint may show through the marker, even the markers billed as "opaque." For example, if you are using a yellow paint for the canvas background and write with a red marker, the lettering may look orange. You can do a test first by painting a little section of the folded-over canvas on the back of the stretcher bars, as you can see in the image in step 5. Once the paint dries, test the pens on your paint color to make sure you like how they look. Or you could skip this step if you want to use a light background and a black pen. If you use a white pen on a dark background as I did in the photos, you definitely will want to go over the letters twice. Totally worth it!

ANOTHER PAINT OPTION

Here's another way to paint the background colors on the canvas. This style of painting adds a whole other dimension to the project:

1. Paint the canvas a solid color that will contrast well with the marker you chose for the lettering. Make sure to paint the edges of the canvas. You can do a couple of coats to get even coverage if you prefer. Let dry.

2. On your palette, mix a little bit of a second paint color with some acrylic gel medium to create a glaze. You want it to be transparent, but with enough color in it that it adds to the piece. Experiment with ratios to see what you like best. Once you have the glaze mixed, paint this liberally all over the canvas, including the sides. Do not let dry.

3. While this second layer is still wet, we're going to remove some of it, which creates a lovely texture and interesting layers of color. Lightly moisten a piece of paper towel with water and scrunch it up into a ball. Gently wipe the paper towel over the center of the canvas to remove some of the glaze. I like to use a circular motion and leave the glaze around the edges of the canvas, which makes it look, depending on the colors, framed, aged, or glowing. Let dry. Repeat as desired until the canvas looks good to you. Trust yourself!

MAP QUOTE

This simple project is so exquisite! Paper vellum, lettered and layered over a map, creates an elegant love note or going-away gift for a friend moving across the country. Instead of a map, you could use also vintage sheet music or other ephemera.

YOU WILL NEED:

- [ ] 8" × 10" clip frame
- [ ] Map page (at least 8" × 10")
- [ ] Pencil
- [ ] Scissors
- [ ] Sheet of translucent paper vellum (available in the scrapbook section of craft stores; it usually comes in 8.5" × 11")
- [ ] Scrap paper
- [ ] Low-tack masking tape
- [ ] Sharpie Oil-Based Paint Marker, black

1 Disassemble the frame and center the glass on top of the map.

2 With a pencil, trace the perimeter of the glass onto the map.

3 Cut away excess map. Repeat with the vellum.

4 Pencil your lettering on scrap paper as a guide. If you want, tape the penciled guide to the table and layer the vellum sheet on top of it. Then also tape down the vellum.

5 Draw your letters with the paint pen. Let dry completely.

6 Carefully remove the tape and layer the vellum over the map. Place glass over map and vellum.

7 Reattach clips to frame.

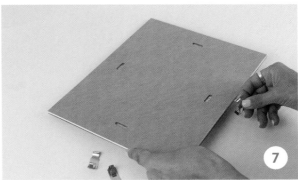

VELLUM OPTIONS

In addition to plain vellum, you can find vellum with subtle prints, which would work perfectly with this project if you want to add another layer of visual interest. If you can't find vellum, or want to just use what you have on hand, try tracing paper. It will be thinner and a bit crinkly, but will have that same frosted look.

WATERCOLOR-RESIST ARTWORK

If you haven't played with watercolors since you were a kid, this is the perfect chance to re-experience their magic. They're simple to use, and the watery intersections of color always look unique.

1. Decide on your phrase or quote. Practice writing it with a pencil on scrap paper to work out the overall layout and spacing. Lightly pencil it in on the watercolor paper.

2. Now it's time to paint the masking fluid over the penciled-in words. After dipping the brush in the fluid, dab it a little on the scrap paper to make sure you don't make puddles or drips on your work. As you continue, try not to paint over what you've done because the liquid will already have started to dry, and the paintbrush will start to rub it off a little bit. If you want to correct any mistakes, just let it dry and rub the masking fluid off in the spot you want to redo. Let dry completely.

3. You can mix up the watercolor with water in the pan and then add it, or you can paint just water all over the paper and then load up the paintbrush with color and drag it across the water you put down. Experiment and have fun. If you haven't played with watercolors before, it's not a bad idea to try it out on scrap paper first.

4   Paint on a light watercolor layer.

5   Add other layers and colors as desired. Be mindful that you don't make your design have too much contrast, because then the lettering won't show up as well. Let dry completely.

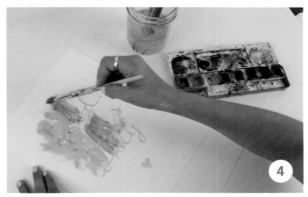

6   Now for my favorite part! With clean fingers, gently rub away at the masking fluid letters, revealing the plain white paper underneath. If you penciled your lettering in before painting, you can erase those guides now. Pop it in a matted frame and you're all set.

BE SURE YOUR ERASER ACTUALLY ERASES

Just to be safe, test your pencil and eraser before you begin to make sure you can easily erase it. Some erasers can leave marks or some faded pencil marks behind. You don't want pencil smudges marring your beautiful work! In a small spot on the back of the watercolor paper, lightly write something and then erase it. If the mark isn't completely removed, try another combination of pencil and eraser until you find the right match.

Chapter 6
HOME ACCENTS

No matter what style you prefer for your home decor—modern, whimsical, antique, country—you'll be able to customize these unique projects to enhance the warmth and personality of your surroundings. Best of all, these eye-catching pieces are quick and easy to make.

PILLOW

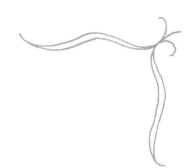

Perking up a room can be as simple as adding new pillows, especially if those pillows are handpainted with your own initials. I love the watercolor look created by using high-flow acrylic paints with plenty of fabric medium (see Chapter 1 for more information).

YOU WILL NEED:

- [ ] Throw pillow with a removable cotton cover
- [ ] Scissors
- [ ] Freezer paper
- [ ] Iron
- [ ] Ironing board (or use a table with a folded towel on it)
- [ ] Optional: scrap paper and pencil
- [ ] Fabric medium
- [ ] Golden High Flow Acrylic paint, aqua, purple, and blue (see sidebar for other color combination suggestions)
- [ ] Scrap cardboard (to use as a palette)
- [ ] Paintbrushes (assorted sizes)
- [ ] Small dish of water

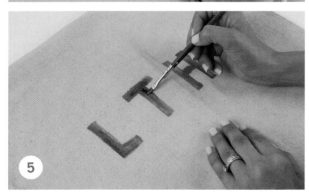

1 Remove the cover from the pillow and turn it inside out.

2 Cut a piece of freezer paper to fit and then iron it, shiny side down, onto the wrong side of the fabric. This will create a backing that will give you a stable surface to paint on, as well as keep the paint from seeping through to the back of the pillow cover. Turn the pillow cover right-side out and gently flatten it out.

3 If desired, practice your design on scrap paper in pencil.

4 Squeeze some fabric medium and the aqua paint onto the scrap cardboard and mix. Start by painting the letters in the center. Take your time and drag the brush over the fabric, giving the paint time to soak into the fabric a little bit.

5 Add the purple paint and more fabric medium to the palette and mix. Dab a little of this mixture into the body of the aqua letters you just painted. This will give a nice mottled watercolor effect.

6   With aqua paint even more thinned with fabric medium, add the shadow to the letters. Pretend that the main letters have a white outline around them that doesn't let the shadows touch the edges of the letters. This gives it that cool floating effect. Start with a line of paint along the edge and then add more fabric medium or a little water to really water down that aqua and fade it into the color of the pillow.

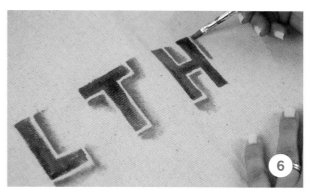

7   With the purple paint and fabric medium mixture, draw the shape around the shadowed letters. Add more paint to blend the shape outward, toward the edges of the pillow, about halfway. You want this to look varied in shades, rather than solidly covering—that's what gives it the look of watercolors. Have fun with it and add more or less fabric medium, depending on how it looks.

8   Starting at the edges of the pillow, add blue paint and fabric medium to blend toward the purple. Continue to thin the paint with fabric medium as needed to get a nice smooth blend.

9   Touch up any areas that you feel need it, but try not to go overboard.

10   Let dry completely and then remove the backing paper. If you need to wash the pillow cover later on, do so by hand with warm water and a mild detergent, and air-dry.

TIPS FOR CHOOSING COLORS

I recommend sticking with a couple of colors that will blend together nicely. Combinations that would work well are generally next to each other on the color wheel, like red (or pink) and orange, which blend together to make a lovely pinkish orange. Another example is the colors in the sample shown—purple and green. Yellow and green would work great, as would green and blue. Try to stay away from color combinations that will get "muddy" when mixed together, such as red and green. You can experiment on scrap paper before you get started, which will help you see what blends well and what suits your personal taste.

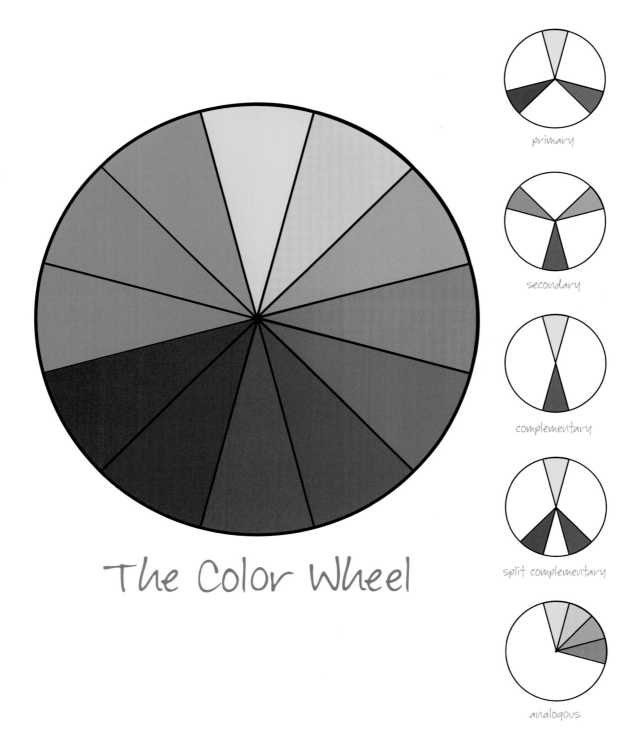

The Color Wheel

primary

secondary

complementary

split complementary

analogous

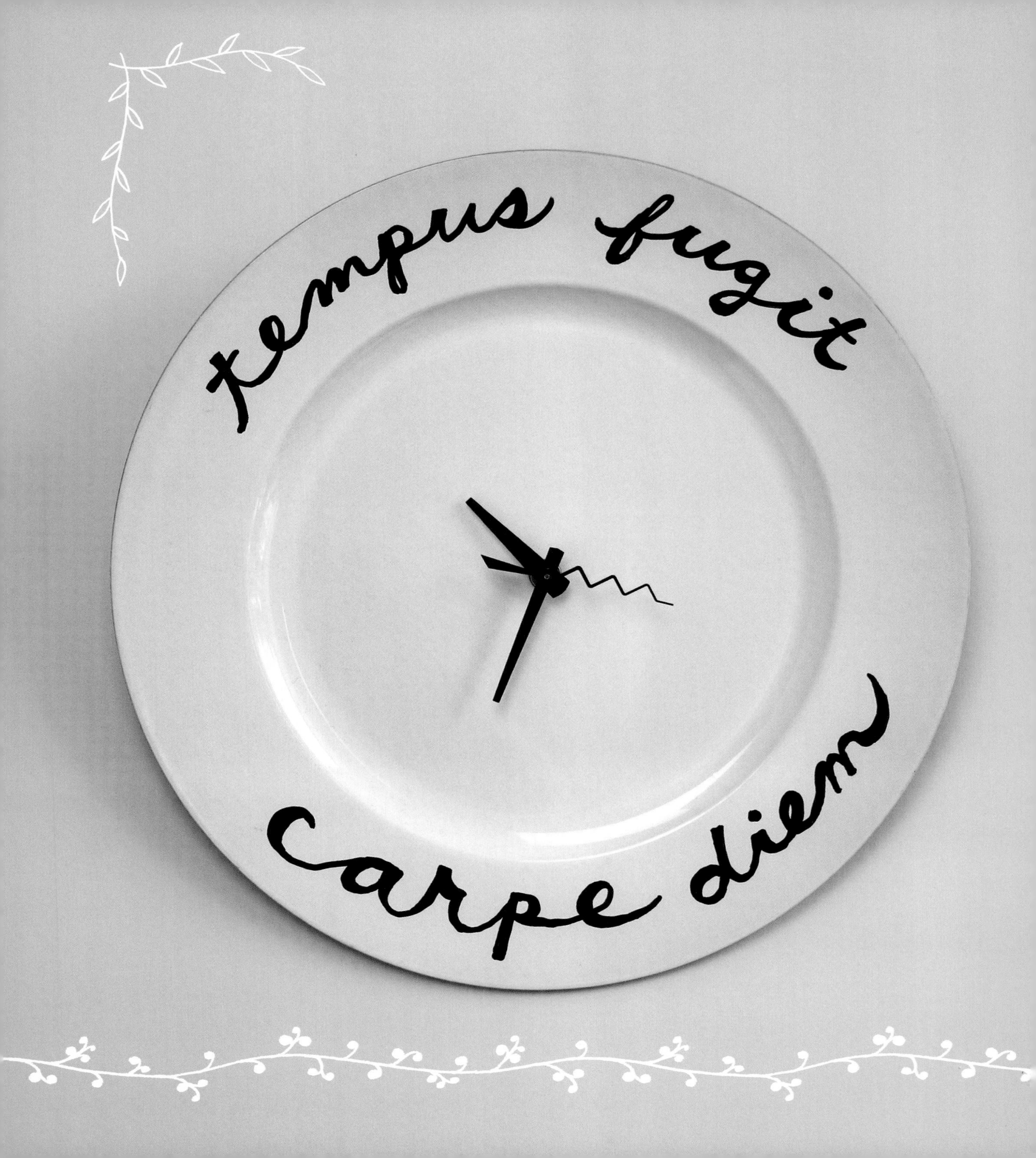
tempus fugit
carpe diem

CLOCK

As you may know, the Latin phrases *tempus fugit* and *carpe diem* translate to "time flies" and "seize the day." As the hours tick by, this one-of-a-kind clock will remind you to enjoy every moment.

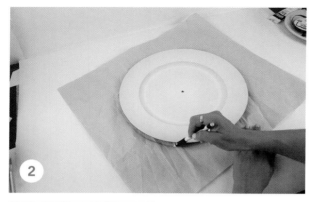

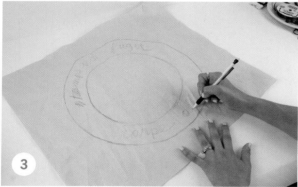

1 Drill a hole in the center of the plate.

2 Place the plate on the newsprint and trace around it. Then take note of how deep the lip is and draw a corresponding line on the newsprint inside the circle to give you a guide for your lettering practice.

3 With your pencil, practice spacing your letters, balancing from left to right and top to bottom. Allow room for the space between each word.

4 Once you have your lettering figured out, it's time to get started with the paint pen. Take note of where you want the line of lettering to begin and space the letters accordingly. Try writing in basic cursive with plenty of space within and between the letters, then go back over to thicken up the "downstrokes."

5 Let dry completely and then attach the clock mechanism according to the manufacturer's instructions.

PRACTICE BEFOREHAND

Keep in mind that with this project, you can't really fix your mistakes. So you will want to practice your lettering enough ahead of time that you feel comfortable just going for it. Since the plastic charger plates are inexpensive, it would be worth it to pick up an extra to practice on. I recommend using a script font for this project because it's much more forgiving than trying to get block lettering to look right with no way to correct it! DON'T ASK ME HOW I KNOW. —Melissa

true love

always

CUSTOMIZED PICTURE FRAME

This frame is so sweet, it will make you want to finally print some of those photos that are taking up all that space on your phone! A couple of coats of paint and some handlettering make this an easy afternoon project to make for your own home or as a gift.

YOU WILL NEED:

- ☐ Unfinished wooden frame (with flat surface to write on)
- ☐ Acrylic paints, a primer, white, and base color of choice
- ☐ Paintbrushes (assorted sizes)
- ☐ Optional: scrap paper
- ☐ Golden High Flow Acrylic paint (color of choice)
- ☐ Fine-grit sandpaper

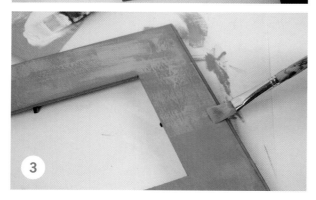

1 Remove the glass and backing from the frame. Prime the frame by painting it white. When dry, paint it with your base color. Don't forget the sides! Let dry.

2 Make the texture color by mixing a bit of white paint with the base paint. You want it to be just slightly lighter than the original color. Use your brush to gently drag some of this paint across the wood.

3 You might find it helpful to first paint onto a scrap piece of paper, taking some of the paint off of the brush first, so that when you go to paint on the frame, the brush is partially dry. This is called dry brushing. This creates depth and visual interest on the surface of the frame. Let dry completely.

4 Draw on your lettering with high-flow acrylic paint and a fine paintbrush.

5 If desired, lightly sand the edges of the picture frame to reveal areas of the base color and the natural wood.

FIND FRAMES ON THE CHEAP

Next time you go to a yard sale or thrift shop, keep your eyes open for inexpensive frames that might work for this project. Look for frames made of wood with a flat surface suitable for lettering. When you get them home, give them a quick clean and layer of primer paint and you are ready to go!

MIRROR

"You look really cute today!" Who doesn't love those words? Get a little boost every time you go to reapply your lipstick with this painted plaque project.

- ☐ Optional: scrap paper
- ☐ Pencil
- ☐ Beveled-edge mirror
- ☐ Wooden plaque (in any size larger than the mirror)
- ☐ Acrylic paint, white and pink (or base color of choice)
- ☐ Paintbrushes
- ☐ Oil-based paint pen (color of choice; try Sharpie Oil-Based Paint Markers)
- ☐ Eclectic E6000 Craft Adhesive
- ☐ Sawtooth hanger

1 Practice your lettering and design on scrap paper if desired.

2 Place the mirror on the plaque in the upper center and trace around it with a pencil. This will give you a guideline to know where to paint.

3 Prime the wood using the white paint. Make sure to get the edges and paint just about ½" into the penciled-in mirror border. Let dry.

4 Paint the wood with pink paint (or color of choice) in the same way. Let dry.

5 Draw on your lettering with the paint pens. Add any other details, dots, borders, or flourishes you like. (See Chapter 3 for ideas.)

6 Use the E6000 to glue the mirror into place. Make sure you get it nice and centered. Let the glue dry as directed on the package.

7 Use E6000 to attach the sawtooth hanger to the back of the plaque.

MAKE IT A PARTY!

These mirrors are a great craft idea for a tween's birthday party or sleepover. Prime all the plaques ahead of time to speed up the process. Let the kids choose their colors and write the words themselves. You glue on the mirrors and hangers while the kids eat pizza and watch a movie!

AREA RUG

Design is everywhere, even underfoot! In this simple project, painted block letters add that personal touch to a basic cotton area rug. This rug will be best used in a low-traffic area, such as next to the bed or in the laundry room.

YOU WILL NEED:

- ☐ Optional: scrap paper and pencil
- ☐ Cotton area rug
- ☐ Sharpie Permanent Marker, black
- ☐ Golden High Flow Acrylic paint, black
- ☐ Fabric medium
- ☐ Paintbrushes (assorted sizes)
- ☐ White acrylic paint

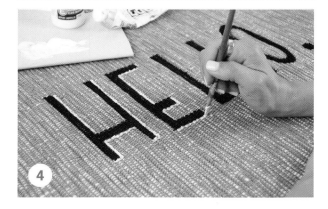

1 Practice your lettering, spacing, and design elements on scrap paper if desired.

2 Lightly outline your letters on the rug with a Sharpie marker. This is just to give you guidelines for painting. You will paint right over these, but be careful not to get marker somewhere that it won't be covered up with paint.

3 Mix the black paint with some fabric medium and fill in the outlines with paint. You might have to take your time and get into all the nooks if your rug is highly textured. Paint over the outlines and make the edges of the letters as crisp as you can.

4 Mix some white paint with the fabric medium and add highlights using a thin brush. If you need to wash the rug after lots of use, do so by hand with warm water and mild detergent, and air-dry.

Chapter 7
WEAR

You don't have to be a jeweler or seamstress to make your own stylish stuff to wear! Skip the mall stores and create your own accessories using words that are meaningful to you.

BRACELET

C'est la vie (the French phrase meaning "that's life") painted in gold script on classic black make this bracelet project *tres chic*. This would be a fun craft for a girls' night in! For an added twist, paint the inside of the bangle a different color.

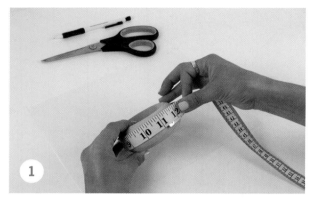

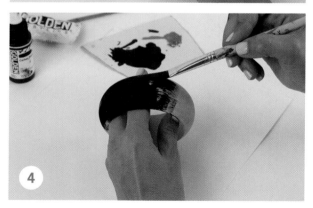

1   Wrap the measuring tape around the outside of the bangle and take note of the length. Measure the height of the bangle.

2   On scrap paper, draw a box that matches the measurements you took. Practice your lettering inside this box, using the lines as a guide. Give yourself plenty of room between your lettering and the top and bottom of the box, as well as a little space where the beginning and end of the lettering meet the box on the sides. This will ensure that when your script is wrapped around the bracelet, it will be spaced correctly.

3   Prime the bangle with white acrylic paint, painting the inside surface first. Lay on wax paper to dry.

4   Paint the bangle black. Let dry completely on the wax paper. If necessary, repeat for better coverage.

5 Now it's time to paint on your phrase. If you aren't accustomed to using a paintbrush for writing, you will want to practice on scrap paper first. Once you are comfortable with it, paint on your phrase using the gold paint. Don't worry too much about making it perfect—it's handlettering, not computer-made! Let the lettering dry. Go back and touch up any areas if you need to.

6 Brush on the acrylic sealer. Let dry.

"I'M SO FANCY" TOTE

You can never have too many cute tote bags. In this project, you'll learn how to quickly dress up a plain canvas tote using lace as a stencil. The options for handlettering a tote bag are endless! Since you will only need to spot-clean this bag, it's okay not to use fabric paint.

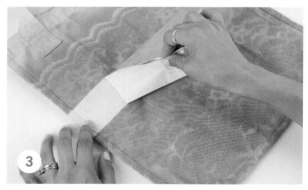

1 Lay the bag flat and tape off the center, where the lettering will go. Press down the edges of the tape with your fingernail to ensure a nice clean line.

2 Take your materials outside and lay the bag on top of the cardboard to both protect the ground from the spray paint and make sure the bag doesn't get dirty. Drape the lace over the bag, leaving a few inches exposed at the top. Smooth out any folds and make sure the lace is lying flat on the canvas.

3 Spray-paint the lace with a few light coats, rather than one heavy coat. Take care to avoid the tote straps as much as possible. You want the spray paint to extend just a little past the lace, but not much further. Let dry completely and then remove the tape.

4 Practice your lettering on paper if desired. Using the fabric marker, take your time and write the phrase in the blank area of canvas that was masked. Add a bold flower pin or your favorites from your button collection if you like!

OTHER OPTIONS

You could use the basic project here to make so many unique crafts. Try bridal party gift bags—spray-paint the bag in your wedding color and write the recipient's name in your prettiest lettering. Or, forego the lace and spray-paint the taped bag. Handletter with "I like big books and I cannot lie" and give to your favorite bookworm, author, or librarian.

LETTERED SHOT-COTTON SCARF

No practice needed for the lettering on this one! This is just your own handwriting—and lots of it—which transforms a piece of cotton into a one-of-a-kind scarf. You can easily customize this for a gift by using a favorite poem or song lyrics that are meaningful to the recipient.

- ☐ 2 yards shot cotton in a dark color (you'll find this at your local fabric shop; this will make 2 scarves)
- ☐ Scissors
- ☐ Clorox Bleach Pen Gel
- ☐ Large piece cardboard
- ☐ Mild soap

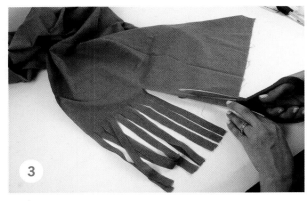

1 Cut the shot cotton in half lengthwise. It will probably already have a pretty strong fold line from its time on the bolt, so go ahead and use that as a guide. Cut off the remaining woven edge of the fabric pieces so all edges are raw. Set aside one of the pieces to make another scarf later.

2 Cut a strip off of one of the short ends of fabric. Practice on this with your bleach pen to get a feel for how it writes.

3 Make a fringe on each end of the scarf fabric by cutting into it about 6" deep and ½" wide.

4 Knot each fringe at the base of the fabric. Once it gets washed, this will fray up nicely.

5 Lay the fabric down on a large piece of cardboard to protect your work surface.

6 Draw on the lettering with the bleach pen. Since this is such a large space of writing, just use your own natural cursive or printing. It's okay if it's not perfect; most of the time it will be wrapped around your neck. The messy nature of the fraying shot cotton will go with any imperfections in your writing. You'll need to work in sections that are about the size of the cardboard. You'll want to work quickly so the bleach at the beginning of the scarf isn't on it for 20 minutes and then the bleach at the end of the scarf is only allowed to set for 2 minutes. Working quickly, you should be able to write on the whole scarf in about 5 minutes.

7 Once the whole scarf is decorated, wait about 20 minutes and then rinse the scarf under warm water. Once you've rinsed off the bleach, wash the scarf by hand with a little mild soap and warm water. Let air-dry. If the fringe has become tangled, pull it apart a little, but don't worry about making it perfect. The crinkly look and loose threads add to the look of this project. Enjoy your bohemian scarf!

WHAT IS SHOT COTTON?

Shot cotton has a lighter, gauzier feel than quilting cotton, and it is woven with two different colors of thread, which gives it a beautiful shifting color. It also frays easily, which is good for us because it provides that tousled, messy look we want in this project.

Use a small piece of this fabric to test out your bleach pen before you do the project. You'll want to get a feel for how much you need to squeeze it and how it writes.

Once you have written on your scarf, you won't be able to tell how much bleaching is happening from the front, but if you gently lift up the fabric, you can see from the back whether the writing is still dark or if it has started to lighten up. I like to leave mine on for about 20 minutes, which bleaches the blue to a nice pink color.

STATEMENT MONOGRAM NECKLACE

It's so much fun to wear jewelry that you've made yourself. This project uses a long ball chain—the length gives the necklace presence, and the ball chain makes it easy to change out the beads later if you want to.

YOU WILL NEED:

- [ ] Toothpick
- [ ] Unfinished wooden pendant (available at craft stores)
- [ ] Acrylic paint, white and colors of choice for base and decorative elements
- [ ] Paintbrushes (assorted sizes)
- [ ] Optional: clear gloss acrylic sealer
- [ ] Large jump ring
- [ ] Round nose pliers
- [ ] Assorted beads with holes large enough to fit on the ball chain
- [ ] Ball chain and closure

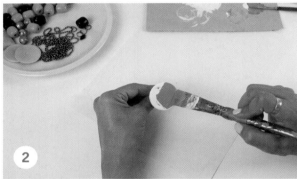

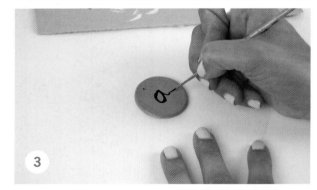

1 Put the toothpick through the hole in the pendant to use as a stand. Paint the wood white to prime it. Make sure to get all around the edges and the back of the pendant. Try not to get paint in the hole.

2 Paint completely with your base color.

3 With a fine brush, paint on the initials.

4 Take your time to add a border or details. You could even make the pendant reversible and draw another design on the other side. Let dry completely and coat with sealer if desired.

5 Open the jump ring with your fingers and round nose pliers. Twist the ends away from each other back and forth, rather than out to the sides. Slip the jump ring through the hole of the pendant. Leave the jump ring open for now and set aside.

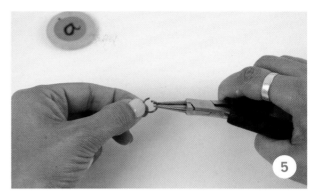

6 Arrange beads as you like on the chain.

7 Slip the jump ring with the pendant on the chain in the middle and close it the same way you opened it (see step 5). Add the closure and you're done!

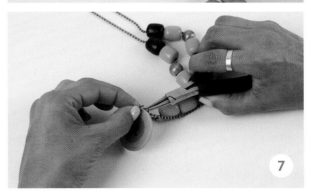

KEYCHAIN

It's so easy to get caught up in your day-to-day to-do lists. Let this key tag be a reminder that wherever you're going, it's good to listen to your heart and "follow your bliss," as Joseph Campbell said.

1. Prime the wooden tag with white acrylic paint. Make sure to get the edges and inside the hole. Don't let the hole fill up with too much paint, though. Try propping the tag on another paintbrush so you don't keep wiping off the paint by handling it. Let dry.

2. Use the Sharpie to write the saying on the tag.

3. Use the oil-based paint pen to add color to the edges of the tag.

4. Open up the split ring and slip the tag onto it. Be careful not to scrape the tag too much with the end of the rings, though it will get scraped up some because the rings are so tight; just touch up the paint as needed.

Chapter 8
HAPPY MAIL

Sure, sending an e-mail is easy, but there's something undeniably special about handwritten words. Reclaim that magic by sending a handwritten note once in a while! Whether it's to a hardworking coworker, loved one, or neighbor, these paper crafts will never fail to bring a smile to someone's face.

ENVELOPES

Sending and receiving "real mail" is such a treat in this digital age. Make it even more of an event by decorating the envelopes with fancy lettering, cool stamps, and washi tape.

YOU WILL NEED:

- [ ] Assortment of envelopes
- [ ] Pencil with eraser
- [ ] Assortment of pens and markers you enjoy using
- [ ] Optional: washi tape, stickers
- [ ] Postage stamps

1 On the front of an envelope, lightly pencil in a large square and divide it with four horizontal lines. This leaves you with five spaces to write in. Think about writing in the center of that space between the lines, rather than on the line. This will give a buffer between each line of lettering.

2 In the first space, write the person's first name in script. Add flourishes as desired.

3 In the second space, write the person's last name in all caps. Depending on the length of her name, you may opt for a tall and skinny letter type or you may write them wide with lots of space between each letter. There is no right or wrong way—just have fun.

4 In the third space, write the street address using large numerals and a short row of capital letters for the street name.

5 In the fourth space, write the city name in script and the state abbreviation in capital letters.

6 In the last space, write the zip code, spreading out the numbers to take up most of the width of the box.

7 Erase your guidelines.

8 Draw a box around your address in pen, if desired. Add decorative flourishes if desired using washi tape, stickers, or drawings. Don't forget to add stamps and your return address before sending to the lucky recipient.

USE INTERESTING POSTAGE

You can further dress up your mail by using pretty postage. Whenever a series of postage stamps comes out that you particularly like, buy a couple of sheets to use on your special mail. The bills can get the basic stuff; use the good stuff for your friends. Stickers and rubber stamps are also fun to use as enhancements. Experiment and have fun with your mail!

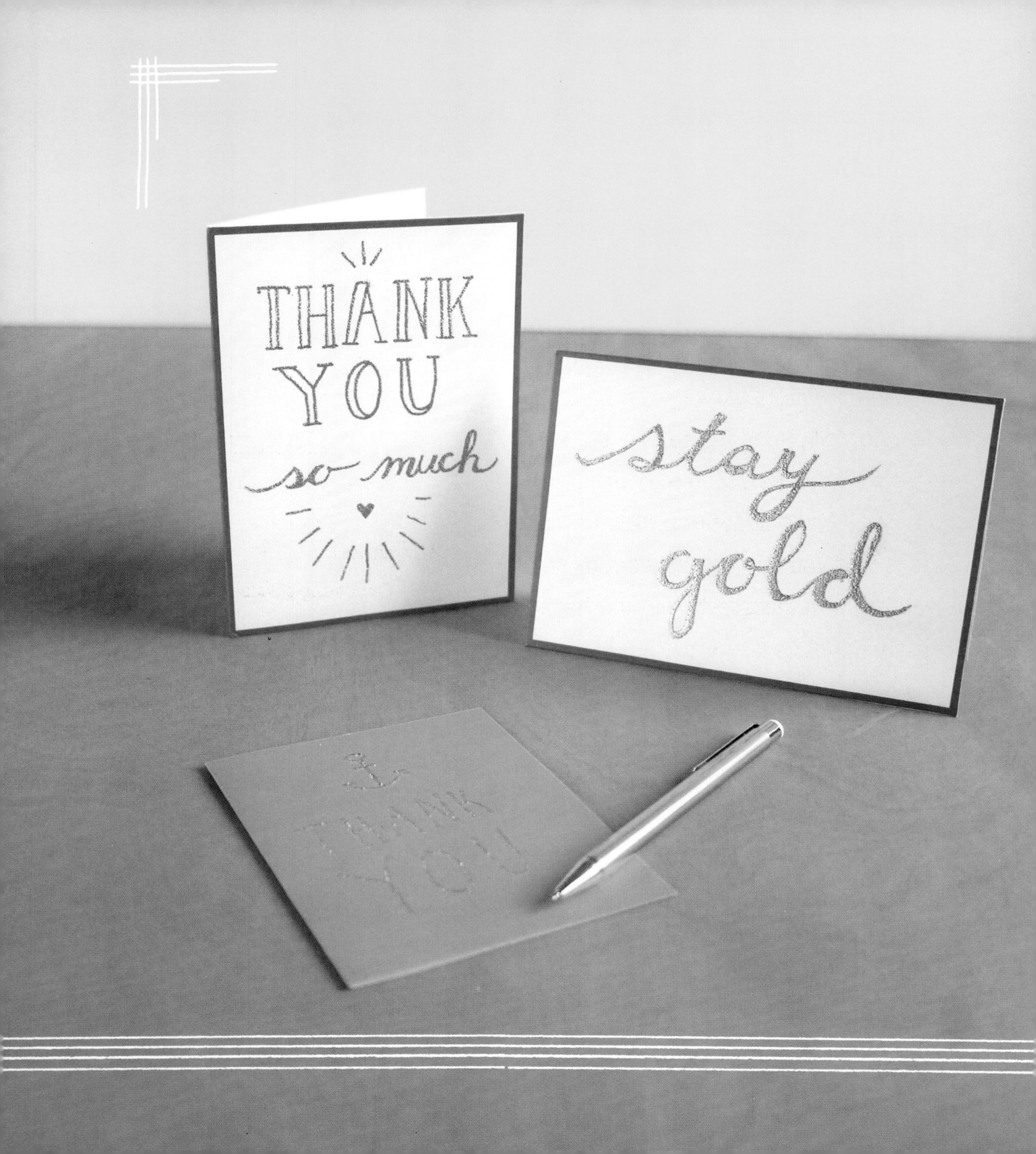
THANK YOU
so much
stay gold
THANK YOU

CARDS

Your handlettering shines even more when you use metallic embossing powders on these handmade cards. Remember: one of the best things about making your own cards is that you can be as sweet or snarky as you like with the greetings! Just because the lettering looks fancy doesn't mean the words can't be irreverent.

YOU WILL NEED:

- ☐ Scrap paper and pencil
- ☐ Blank cards
- ☐ Embossing pen (color of choice)
- ☐ Embossing powder (color of choice)
- ☐ Heat tool (available in craft stores; you'll find it with the embossing pens and powders)

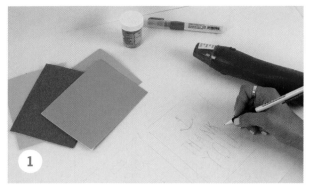

1 Practice your lettering, layout, and any flourishes or borders on scrap paper with a pencil.

2 Once you are happy with your design, pencil it in on a card.

3 With the embossing pen, draw over your letters and design elements. The clear liquid in the embossing pen stays wet for a little while, just long enough to sprinkle on the embossing powder, so work quickly.

4 Lay a sheet of scrap paper under the card and pour the embossing powder over the wet lettering. Make sure you get a bunch all over everything that's wet. You'll have a pile of powder, probably a tablespoon's worth, or two.

5 Hold the card up and let the excess embossing powder fall onto the paper. If a bunch of extra powder stays on the card by static, that's okay; just give the card a little tap or flick with your finger to shake it off. Don't do this too hard or it will get dislodged from where you want it, adhered to the embossing liquid. If this does happen, that's okay; just sprinkle some more on and tap off the excess a little lighter this time.

6   If your card is made of textured card stock, you may find that grains of the powder stick in the little indents. Just use a dry paintbrush to dislodge them. Or stay away from textured papers if you know this will make you crazy. Once you are finished with the embossing powder, make a crease in the scrap paper lengthwise to act as a "funnel" and pour the excess powder back in the jar.

7   Now the fun part! Lay the card flat on a heat-safe surface and turn on the heat tool. Hold the end of the tool 1"–2" away from the card (check the manufacturer's instructions, as this may vary from tool to tool) and gently go back and forth above the design. Don't stay in one place too long. After a few seconds, you'll notice that the embossing powder starts to react to the heat by melting or bubbling, creating the raised and shiny surface known as embossing. Once the design is uniformly heated and embossed, you're done!

8   If you're using white paper, try edging your cards in a color to make them pop.

TIPS ON WORKING WITH EMBOSSING POWDER

Embossing powder melts and expands when the heat tool is used on it. It is like magic, watching the heat work and the powder bubble and shine before your eyes. Since it does expand a little, you want to make sure you give your letters a little bit of "space" to allow room for the transformation from powder to shiny raised lettering.

WOODEN POSTCARD

Once you try woodburning, you are going to want to "burn" everything. Get your fix by inscribing a greeting into a wooden postcard. Definitely practice on scrap wood first. This unexpected correspondence is a sure hit with any recipient!

YOU WILL NEED:

- [ ] Woodburning tool
- [ ] Ceramic mug (to use as a heat-safe holder for the tool)
- [ ] Scrap wood (for practicing)
- [ ] Scrap paper and pencil
- [ ] Optional: ruler
- [ ] 3½" × 5" wooden postcard, available at craft stores

1 First, let's practice. Place the tip-end of the tool in the mug and plug it in. Take your time and practice on the scrap wood. This will help you get a sense of how long to hold the tool on the wood, how hard to press, and what kind of marks are created by holding the tool at different angles. Some tools come with different metal tips to attach to get different line qualities. Try it all out to see how it feels. Practice drawing some letters.

2 Trace the wooden postcard onto a piece of scrap paper so you can create your design.

3 Now that you have a sense of how it feels to use the tool, practice lettering with a pencil on the paper, keeping that in mind. If you like bolder, thicker lines, you don't want to use a fine, double-lined font, right? If you are comfortable with burning thin, curved lines, then feel free to use those kinds of letters in your design. To get the stretched-out look of these letters, I drew in some lines as guides using a ruler. First I marked off a ½" border all around the edge. Then I drew my diagonal line to separate the basic shapes. I added a border above and below this line as well, to create a buffer zone so my letters wouldn't run into each other. Then I drew a line in each half from the pointed end to the center of the opposite side—this is the line to keep the horizontal lines of the letters aligned to.

This might feel familiar if you ever drew one-point perspective in art class. Now to make the letters, just keep the vertical parts of the letters going straight up and down as usual, but end them at the border lines, and make the horizontal lines of the letters follow the other guidelines.

4 Redraw your final design in pencil on the wood postcard.

5 Use the woodburning tool to burn over your penciled-in lines. This is not one of those instant projects, so take your time and enjoy the process. Be mindful of the metal disk below the tip of the tool—it's easy to inadvertently burn the wood with it.

MAILING WOODEN POSTCARDS

While you could actually send this postcard through the mail as is, you might consider popping it in an envelope first. You'll definitely want to bring this to the post office to make sure that it gets weighed so you can apply the proper postage. Also write DO NOT BEND on the envelope and ask the clerk to hand-cancel it.

PERSONALIZED JOURNALS

Whether you need to get things off your chest or out of your brain, writing things down is a great way to do it. Keep track of your evil plans (or good deeds) with these easy-to-make personalized journals.

YOU WILL NEED:

- [ ] Scrap paper and pencil
- [ ] Journals with plain covers
- [ ] Sharpie Permanent Marker (color of choice), fine point

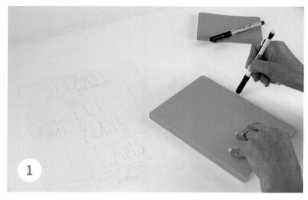

1. Trace the shape of your journal onto scrap paper with a pencil so you have the correct dimensions.

2. Practice your ideas on the paper. You can design a whole, full cover with lots of detail and flourishes or you could keep it minimal with just a couple of words. Once you get the layout you like and have chosen your lettering styles, you can jump into decorating.

3. Using your penciled layout as a guide, draw your lettering on the cover with your fine-point Sharpie. If the surface of your journal is porous, you may need to go over your lettering twice.

4. Add details, borders, and flourishes as desired (see Chapter 3 for ideas).

OTHER IDEAS

You could use these same instructions and customize all kinds of different blank books for gifts or personal use. Think about fun phrases you could handletter on the cover of guest books (I Was Here, John Hancocks), photo albums (Rogue's Gallery, Photos That Aren't on My Phone), and sketchbooks (Bad Ideas, Kinda Sketchy)—or keep it simple and write the recipient's initials.

STATIONERY

For a letter to a special person, try creating your own handlettered stationery. This is a great chance to incorporate some of the banners or flourishes from Chapter 3.

- ☐ Scrap paper
- ☐ Pencil with eraser
- ☐ Lightweight card stock
- ☐ Pigma Micron Pen, fine point

1. Practice your banners and lettering layouts on scrap paper. Once you feel comfortable with it, pencil it in on the card stock.

2. Take your time and draw the design in with the pen. Don't think about exactly tracing the design; rather you are using the penciled lines as a guide for your own fluid drawing. You should feel free to edit and adjust on the fly.

3. Erase pencil lines and write someone a heartfelt letter!

THE MORE,
THE MERRIER

It's always nice to do these by hand for someone in particular, but sometimes you just want to be able to use some already-made stationery in a pinch. If you are computer savvy, scan in your original and print it out on card stock to make multiples of the same design. You can use them as is or you could experiment with adding color with watercolor paints or markers. You'll feel freer to do so because you won't be worried about "ruining" the original.

INDEX